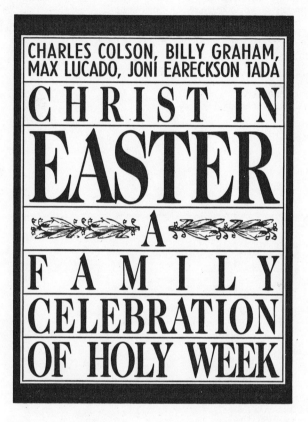

CHARLES COLSON, BILLY GRAHAM,
MAX LUCADO, JONI EARECKSON TADA

CHRIST IN
EASTER

A

FAMILY
CELEBRATION
OF HOLY WEEK

NAVPRESS

A MINISTRY OF THE NAVIGATORS
P.O. BOX 6000, COLORADO SPRINGS, COLORADO 80934

The Navigators is an international Christian organization. Jesus Christ gave His followers the Great Commission to go and make disciples (Matthew 28:19). The aim of The Navigators is to help fulfill that commission by multiplying laborers for Christ in every nation.

NavPress is the publishing ministry of The Navigators. NavPress publications are tools to help Christians grow. Although publications alone cannot make disciples or change lives, they can help believers learn biblical discipleship, and apply what they learn to their lives and ministries.

Library of Congress Catalog Card Number 90-60399
ISBN 08910-93095

Second printing, paperback edition, 1991

Cover illustration: Phil Boatwright
Inside illustrations: C.B. Mordan

Compiled and edited by Cheryl Stine.

The Innocent Prisoner by Charles Colson is adapted from the Prisoner Tract. Used by permission of Prison Fellowship Ministries.

We Too Shall Live by Billy Graham, from April 1973 DECISION magazine, © 1973 Billy Graham Evangelistic Association. Used by permission.

Unless otherwise identified, all Scripture quotations in this publication are from the *Holy Bible: New International Version* (NIV). Copyright © 1973, 1978, 1984, International Bible Society. Used by permission of Zondervan Bible Publishers. Another version used is the *King James Version.*

Printed in the United States of America

Contents

Introduction

Easter should be a day of unsurpassed joy and celebration. Without the Resurrection there is no Christianity. From the Cross, Jesus cried, "It is finished!" On the following Sunday this was confirmed with the resounding "Amen!" of the Resurrection. The price had been paid for our sins and the sacrifice had been accepted. Jesus conquered death and sin. In Him we, too, are victorious.

This book will enable your family to experience this Easter joy in a new way. Through devotional and Scripture readings, hymns, poems, family discussions, and activities, your family will come to a better understanding of the events surrounding the death and resurrection of Jesus Christ. In the process, family bonds will be strengthened as you see how the stories of Holy Week are relevant to all of life.

Traditionally, a forty-day period of preparation called Lent has preceded Easter. For many people this period is characterized by fasting and self-denial. The tradition of forty days is believed to have come from the forty days Jesus spent in the wilderness before He began His public ministry. This book is not designed to cover the entire period of Lent, but covers the eight days from Palm Sunday to Easter. It provides a way for your family to prepare for Easter, day by day through Holy Week, with an emphasis on worship and fun times together.

This book includes four main sections: Palm Sunday, the Last Supper (Thursday),

Good Friday, and Easter. There are also four shorter lessons for the other days of Holy Week. Each session offers you a choice of activities to do together as a family. Some are very simple, others are more involved. It will be helpful if one family member looks ahead at the activity suggestions and gathers the things needed for the activities your family is most likely to enjoy. If the age span of your children is large, you may want to choose a different activity for each child.

Included in each of the four main sessions are additional readings. These scriptures, poems, and shorter devotional pieces are meant to be used if time allows. Parents may choose to read these on their own.

As you see the events of Holy Week unfold day by day, you will get a fresher sense of the mystery and meaning of Easter and how it can change your life. May the Resurrection life of the Lord fill you as you draw closer to Him this Easter.

Happy Celebration!

—The Publisher

THE STORY'S NOT OVER YET

MAX LUCADO has served as a minister in St. Louis and Miami and as a missionary in Rio de Janeiro, Brazil. He is presently pulpit minister of Oak Hills Church of Christ in San Antonio, Texas. His books include *On the Anvil, No Wonder They Call Him the Savior, God Came Near,* and *Six Hours One Friday.*

S P E C I A L   E A S T E R   S E A S O N   M E S S A G E

The Story's Not Over Yet

BY MAX LUCADO

The message of Easter is clear—the story's not over yet. We haven't heard the punchline, and we haven't finished the battle. Don't be premature in your judgments or too final in your opinion. The Judge hasn't returned, and the jury isn't in.

The story isn't over yet. All that needs to be said hasn't been said. And all that will be seen hasn't been seen.

That's good news. If your eyes have ever moistened at the newsreels of the hungry, remember the story's not over yet. If you've ever been bewildered as you beheld pain triumph over peace—keep the Easter message in mind. The story's not over yet.

If you've ever found your fists clinched in rage as you read of the atrocities at Auschwitz, I've got something to show you. If you've stood distraught as you hear stories of yet another hijacking . . . another serial murderer . . . another child beating, there is a verse I want you to consider.

Or perhaps your feelings are more personal. Maybe the ugly moments in history and open wounds of our day have dared to leave your television screen and enter your house.

Maybe you've buried a child whose body was broken by a reckless driver. Maybe your child has never called you daddy. Maybe the one who promised to love you forever loved you for only as long as it was convenient. Maybe you've suffered personally from the cruelties in the world. Maybe the shadow of the question mark has blackened your door.

Maybe you have asked "Why?"

"The rain on the unjust I can understand . . . but why the just?" "To suffer the consequences of my sins makes sense, but why should I pay for the sin of others?" "Why the innocent?" "Why the children?" "Why the pure?" "Why me?"

Hard questions. Necessary questions. Questions surfaced by a perplexing passage in Matthew.

Is there any passage in Scripture bloodier than the killing of the children by the soldiers of Herod? Though not specifically described, its bloody footprints are left between the lines of these verses.

When Herod realized that he had been outwitted by the Magi, he was furious, and he gave orders to kill all the boys in Bethlehem and its vicinity who were two years old and under, in accordance with the time he had learned from the Magi. Then what was said through the prophet Jeremiah was fulfilled:

> "A voice is heard in Ramah,
>> weeping and great mourning,
> Rachel weeping for her children
>> and refusing to be comforted,
> because they are no more."   (Matthew 2:16-18)

It's a grisly scene: horses galloping, mothers with small boys running and screaming. The flashing of weapons. The flow of innocent blood. The sudden stillness of tiny hands.

Mothers clutching lifeless bodies to blood-soaked breasts.

It's a scene of swords piercing the innocent.

No justification. No explanation. Just cruel carnage. A senseless slaughter.

And during it all, a fat king sits on a throne less than ten miles away, blind to the tears he has summoned, deaf to the anguish he has caused. Herod drinks wine the color of the blood he is spilling.

The wail heard in Bethlehem echoes through the stars. A chorus of chaos refusing to be comforted. A thousand tears with one voice, a hundred hearts with one question.

"Why?"

□ □ □

The composer of this chaos watches from a nearby mountain. With each flash of the sword, he claps. With each plunge of the dagger, he gloats.

Evil at its worst. Blackness at its darkest.

This madman sheds no tears for the young-dead. He is intent on only one thing: killing the Christ before He leaves the cradle.

And when the ravage is completed and the madman knows he has failed, he curses, swirls around, and returns to his pit.

□ □ □

Thirty years later, the other moment for which Satan has waited arrives. He is repeating his drama of desolation. Once again he is slaughtering the innocent.

Once again swords flash and feet scamper. Once again a spineless king called Herod is a pawn in the play. Once again there are the tears of a mother who wonders why. Once again flesh is torn. Once again there are the cries of anguish.

Once again Satan is trying to kill life itself.

S P E C I A L   E A S T E R   S E A S O N   M E S S A G E

This time he has Him where he wants Him. God on a cross. The One who escaped him in Bethlehem is bolted to a tree. Satan applauds as the skin is ripped. "This time You won't get away!"

A spear breaks through Jesus' ribs. Once again the innocent is pierced.

"I have done it!" The madman dances amidst the demons. "I have won!"

But his claim is premature.

For the crucified One who descends the spiral stairway into the cavern of death is not a defeated messiah. And He has not come to surrender. Far from it. He is a creator, and He has come to reclaim His own.

He has come to storm the gates of death.

He scatters the demons and rips open the prison doors. He takes captivity captive and frees the faithful.

You can be sure of one thing. Among the voices that sing His welcome are His Bethlehem brothers. They died that He might escape. He has now died that they might escape. They died that He might live. And now, He's returned to return the favor.

The Easter announcement is clear. Victory is secure. Wails of Bethlehem will turn into the victories of Calvary. Don't forget that.

The next time the soldiers of Satan steal the joy from your arms.

The next time your prayers float into a silent sky.

The next time you wonder how God could sit still while the innocent suffer.

Remember, the story's not over yet. Remember the Easter Jesus rescued the imprisoned and remember . . . He is coming to do it again.

SPECIAL EASTER SEASON MESSAGE

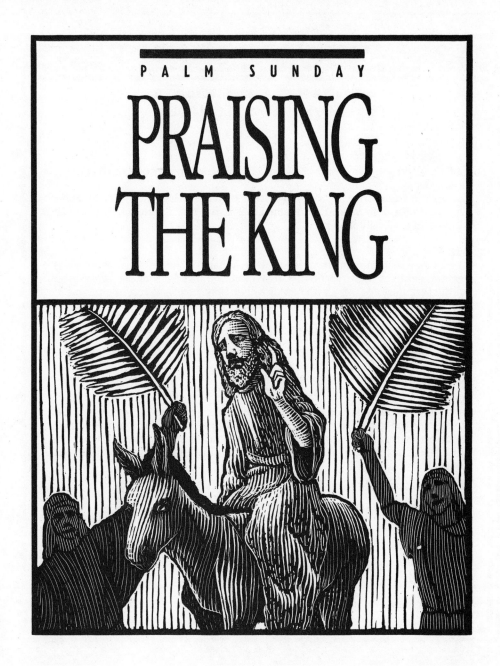

PALM SUNDAY'S SCRIPTURE

OPENING THOUGHTS

☐ What would you do to honor the President if you heard that he would be driving down your street tomorrow?

☐ The word *hosanna* means "save now." It came from two Hebrew words that were a cry to God for deliverance (see Psalm 118:25). By New Testament times it had become an exclamation of praise.

MATTHEW 21:1-9

As they approached Jerusalem and came to Bethphage on the Mount of Olives, Jesus sent two disciples, saying to them, "Go to the village ahead of you, and at once you will find a donkey tied there, with her colt by her. Untie them and bring them to me. If anyone says anything to you, tell him that the Lord needs them, and he will send them right away."

This took place to fulfill what was spoken through the prophet:

"Say to the Daughter of Zion,
    'See, your king comes to you,
gentle and riding on a donkey,
    on a colt, the foal of a donkey.'"

The disciples went and did as Jesus had instructed them. They brought the donkey and the colt, placed their cloaks on them, and Jesus sat on them. A very large crowd spread their cloaks on the road, while others cut branches from the trees and spread them on the road. The crowds that went ahead of him and those that followed shouted.

"Hosanna to the Son of David!"

"Blessed is he who comes in the name of the Lord!"

"Hosanna in the highest!"

LUKE 19:39-40

Some of the Pharisees in the crowd said to Jesus, "Teacher, rebuke your disciples!"

"I tell you," he replied, "if they keep quiet, the stones will cry out."

ALL GLORY, LAUD AND HONOR

All glory, laud, and honor
To Thee, Redeemer, King,
To whom the lips of children
Made sweet hosannas ring:
Thou art the King of Israel,
Thou David's royal Son,
Who in the Lord's name comest,
The King and blessed one!

The company of angels
Are praising Thee on high,
And mortal men and all things
Created make reply:
The people of the Hebrews
With palms before Thee went;
Our praise and prayer and anthems
Before Thee we present.

To Thee, before Thy passion,
They sang their hymns of praise;
To Thee, now high exalted,
Our melody we raise:
Thou didst accept their praises—
Accept the praise we bring,
Who in all good delightest,
Thou good and gracious King!

Theodulph of Orleans, Author and Composer
John M. Neale, Translator

The Welcome

esus was welcomed by an enthusiastic crowd that Sunday two thousand years ago. "He was a King; royal, without trappings. His garment was homemade . . . His steed was a beast of burden not yet broken to harness . . . His courtiers were fisherfolk, His cavalcade a mob of Galileans. And yet no pageant that ever passed through the streets of imperial Rome has so impressed the centuries as that. The triumphal entries of Roman emperors are almost forgotten, but of that entry of Jesus to Jerusalem, every detail recorded is known by the common people everywhere" (G. Campbell Morgan).

Jesus entered Jerusalem as King, but the crowds that greeted Him didn't understand that His Kingdom was not of this world. Likewise, Jesus stands ready to enter every corridor of our lives, and yet we fail to understand and give Him complete access. "A spiritual kingdom lies all about us, enclosing us, embracing us, altogether within reach of our inner selves, waiting for us to recognize it. God Himself is here waiting our response to His presence. This eternal world will come alive to us the moment we begin to reckon upon its reality" (A. W. Tozer).

Are you ready to welcome Jesus? Do you want the spiritual world to be real to you? Are you willing to give the King entry into every aspect of your life?

"It all hinges upon Jesus coming into the heart as His own house—altogether His own. If there are some rooms of which we do not give up the key—some little sitting-room which we would like to keep as a little mental retreat, with a view from the window, which we do not quite want to give up—some lodger whom we would rather not send away just yet—some little dark closet which we have no resolution to open and set right—of course the King has not full possession; our heart is not all and really His own. . . . Only throw open all the doors, and the King of glory shall come in" (Frances Ridley Havergal).

Are you like the people in the fickle crowd who greeted Jesus on Palm Sunday, but turned their backs when it seemed inconvenient and unprofitable to follow Him on Friday?

This Easter week, open all the doors of your life and welcome Jesus with outstretched arms. Uproot the weeds of discontent and pull out the briers of deceit from your life, and offer them as palm branches. Take off the layers of pretense and the robes of self-centeredness that smother your heart, and lay them at the feet of Jesus.

"Give to Christ, therefore, free entrance into your heart, and keep out all things that hinder His entrance. When you have Him, you are rich enough, and He alone will be sufficient for you. Then He will be your provider and defender and your faithful helper in every necessity" (Thomas á Kempis).

Today and throughout this Holy Week, join all creation in unhindered praise and welcome to the Triumphal King.

Sources for this devotional were: G. Campbell Morgan, The Gospel According to Matthew *(Fleming H. Revell); A. W. Tozer,* The Pursuit of God *(Christian Publications, Inc.); Frances Ridley Havergal,* Opened Treasures *(Loizeaux Brothers); and Thomas á Kempis,* The Imitation of Christ, *translated by Richard Whitford, edited by Harold C. Gardiner (Doubleday & Company, Inc.).*

PALM SUNDAY / PRAISING THE KING

1. Imagine for a minute that Jesus is coming to spend the day with you tomorrow. What would you change about your day? Would you start your day differently? Would you go different places, talk to different people, or maybe spend your money differently?
2. Since Jesus really is with you all the time, what parts of your life would you like to change? Identify one specific thing that you can work on in the next week.
3. The crowd that greeted Jesus had a sense of anticipation and excitement. What are you looking forward to in the next week as you celebrate Easter as a family?
4. Many of the people who met Jesus beside the road to Jerusalem expected Him to free them from the oppression of Roman rulers. But God had a different plan, a greater plan—a plan to free all mankind from the penalty and oppression of sin. Are there some things you are expecting of Jesus that may not be part of God's best plan for you?

ADDITIONAL READING

A man can no more diminish God's glory by refusing to worship Him than a lunatic can put out the sun by scribbling the word "darkness" on the walls of his cell.

C. S. Lewis, 1898-1963

THE PALMS

O'er all the way, green palms and blossoms gay
Are strewn, this day, in festal preparation,
Where Jesus comes, to wipe our tears away
E'en now the throng to welcome Him prepare:

Join all and sing, His name declare,
Let ev'ry voice resound with acclamation,
Hosanna! Praised be the Lord!
Bless Him who cometh to bring salvation!

His word goes forth, and peoples by its might
Once more regain freedom from degradation,
Humanity doth give to each his right,
While those in darkness find restored the light!

PALM SUNDAY / PRAISING THE KING

Join all and sing, His name declare,
Let ev'ry voice resound with acclamation,
Hosanna! Praised be the Lord!
Bless Him who cometh to bring salvation!

Sing and rejoice, oh, blest Jerusalem,
Of all thy sons sing the emancipation,
Through boundless love the Christ of Bethlehem
Brings faith and hope to thee for evermore.

Join all and sing, His name declare,
Let ev'ry voice resound with acclamation,
Hosanna! Praised be the Lord!
Bless Him who cometh to bring salvation!

Jean-Baptiste Faure, 1830-1914

F A M I L Y   A C T I V I T I E S

Make a family Praise Tree. You will need:
- ☐ Small branch without leaves
- ☐ Tin can big enough to hold the branch
- ☐ Small rocks
- ☐ Construction paper to make leaves
- ☐ Wire or ribbon
- ☐ Colored tissue paper or ribbon scraps
- ☐ Pens or pencils

1. Place the branch inside the tin can. Put the rocks around the branch to fill the can.
2. Add some colorful decoration to your Praise Tree. Cut several 1″ x 2″ pieces of tissue paper. Gather each piece of paper together in the middle, and attach it to the tree with a piece of string or ribbon.
3. Cut the construction paper in the shape of leaves that are big enough to write a few words on.
4. Have family members write down one simple praise to God on each leaf. These Scripture verses may give you ideas: Psalm 8:1, Psalm 36:5-9, Psalm 103:1-2. Also include specific praises from your lives.
5. Punch a hole through the end of each leaf with a pencil and tie the leaves on the tree with pieces of wire or ribbon.
6. As friends and family come to visit, ask them if they would like to add some leaves of

praise to your tree. Be sure to have extra leaves ready to use for this purpose. Family members may also wish to add to the tree throughout the week.

□ □ □

Make a Psalm Palm. You will need:
- □ Large piece of white paper
- □ Two or three pieces of green paper
- □ Glue
- □ Crayons or markers

1. Cut narrow strips from the green paper in the shape of individual palm leaves. Each family member should write a few short sentences, praising God for who He is and what He has done. Be specific about what God has done in your life recently.
2. Glue the narrow leaves onto the white paper so that together they form the shape of a palm branch.
3. Put your poster up somewhere as a reminder of God's blessings in your life. When Easter is over save this poster for next year. A year from now, it will be fun to see what each person wrote.

□ □ □

Start a Picture Poster for the days of Holy Week. You will add a new picture each day. This will help small children remember what you talked about each day, and will build anticipation and curiosity for what is coming next. You will need:
- □ Piece of posterboard, or a large piece of paper
- □ Plain white paper for drawings
- □ Markers, crayons, or pencils
- □ Glue

1. Divide the posterboard or large piece of paper into eight equal boxed sections—one for each of the days from Palm Sunday up to and including Easter.
2. Have each child draw one picture of a small palm leaf. These must all fit into the first box.
3. Glue the palm leaves in the first box, and put the poster where it is easily accessible throughout the week. You will add an appropriate drawing every day of Holy Week.

□ □ □

Check out several art books from your local library. Spend time together as a family looking at the great works of art portraying the events of Holy Week. Here are some titles to look for:

Christ and the Fine Arts by Cynthia Pearl Maus
The Life of Christ in Masterpieces of Art compiled by Marvin Ross
The Dore Bible Illustrations by Gustave Dore
The Bible and Its Painters by Bruce Bernard

□ □ □

Check your library or music store for recordings of classical music written for Easter. Look for these works:

Requiem by John Rutter
St. Matthew Passion by Johann Sebastian Bach
Easter Oratorio by Johann Sebastian Bach
Requiem by Wolfgang Amadeus Mozart
A German Requiem by Johannes Brahms
Five Mystical Songs: Rise Heart (Easter) by Ralph Vaughan Williams

Hosanna to Christ

Hosanna to the royal son
Of David's ancient line!
His natures two, his person one,
Mysterious and divine.

The root of David, here we find,
And offspring, are the same:
Eternity and time are joined
In our Immanuel's name.

Blest he that comes to wretched man
With peaceful news from Heaven!
Hosannas, of the highest strain,
To Christ the Lord be given.

Let mortals ne'er refuse to take
The Hosanna on their tongues,
Lest rocks and stones should rise and break
Their silence into songs.

Isaac Watts, 1674-1748

P R A Y E R

Lord Jesus,
We want to open our hearts completely to You in welcome this week. Help us to do this. We confess that there are areas of our lives we would rather hide from You. Even if this were possible, we know that holding back from You only hurts us. We are helpless, Lord. We ask You to fill our lives. Help us even in our unwillingness to give You entry into our hearts. Amen.

MONDAY

CLEANSING THE TEMPLE

TUESDAY

QUESTIONING JESUS

WEDNESDAY

THE ANOINTING OF JESUS

CLEANSING THE TEMPLE

OPENING THOUGHTS

☐ Think about your childhood. Can you recall a time when you understood some situation better than the adults did? What did you do? Were you able to help the grownups see your perspective?

☐ People came from many miles away to worship God at the Temple in Jerusalem during the Passover celebration. Money changers were in the Temple exchanging the people's local currency for the proper currency to pay the Temple tax. There were also vendors selling animals for the people to use as sacrifices. The merchants and the money changers were cheating the people. The Court of the Gentiles, where all this buying and selling was taking place, was supposed to be a place for the Gentiles to worship and pray to God. Instead, it had become a wild and noisy place filled with dishonesty.

MATTHEW 21:12-17

Jesus entered the temple area and drove out all who were buying and selling there. He overturned the tables of the money changers and the benches of those selling doves. "It is written," he said to them, " 'My house will be called a house of prayer,' but you are making it a 'den of robbers.'"

The blind and the lame came to him at the temple, and he healed them. But when the chief priests and the teachers of the law saw the wonderful things he did and the children shouting in the temple area, "Hosanna to the Son of David," they were indignant.

"Do you hear what these children are saying?" they asked him.

"Yes," replied Jesus, "have you never read,

" 'From the lips of children and infants you have ordained praise'?"

And he left them and went out of the city to Bethany, where he spent the night.

DISCUSSION AND REFLECTION

1. What made the chief priests and teachers of the law angry?
2. What made Jesus angry?
3. Why do you think the religious leaders overlooked the sin and irreverence in their midst, yet became angry about Jesus healing the blind and lame and the children singing praises to Him?
4. Read these verses out loud: "Don't you know that you yourselves are God's temple and that God's Spirit lives in you? If anyone destroys God's temple, God will destroy him; for God's temple is sacred, and you are that temple" (1 Corinthians 3:16-17). What cleaning needs to be done in your "temple"?

FAMILY ACTIVITIES

☐ Do some research on the Temple. Find out who built the Temple of Jesus' day and when it was built.

☐ Add a new picture to your Picture Poster, which was started on Palm Sunday. Have each child draw a simple picture of a child praising Jesus in the Temple. Put these drawings in the second box on the poster.

PRAYER

Have a child read the prayer today.

Dear Lord,

Thank You that I can love and serve You while I am young. Help me to keep my life pure for You. Amen.

QUESTIONING JESUS

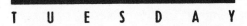

OPENING THOUGHTS

☐ If you could have a face-to-face talk with Jesus, what would you ask Him?

☐ Tuesday of Holy Week was one of the busiest days in Jesus' ministry on earth. He went to the Temple in Jerusalem early. There He was asked one difficult question after another. He amazed the religious leaders with His perfect answers. Finally, He asked them a question that showed that they had no understanding of what the Scriptures said about the Messiah. After this humiliation, the leaders were silenced.

MATTHEW 22:34-46

Hearing that Jesus had silenced the Sadducees, the Pharisees got together. One of them, an expert in the law, tested him with this question: "Teacher, which is the greatest commandment in the Law?"

Jesus replied: " 'Love the Lord your God with all your heart and with all your soul and with all your mind.' This is the first and greatest commandment. And the second is like it: 'Love your neighbor as yourself.' All the Law and the Prophets hang on these two commandments."

While the Pharisees were gathered together, Jesus asked them, "What do you think about the Christ? Whose son is he?"

"The son of David," they replied.

He said to them, "How is it then that David, speaking by the Spirit, calls him 'Lord'? For he says,

"'The Lord said to my Lord:
"Sit at my right hand
until I put your enemies
under your feet."'

If then David calls him 'Lord,' how can he be his son?" No one could say a word in reply, and from that day on no one dared to ask him any more questions.

DISCUSSION AND REFLECTION
1. How are the two greatest commandments related to each other?
2. Which of these commandments is harder for you to keep?
3. What question do you think Jesus might want to ask *you* at this point in your life?

FAMILY ACTIVITIES
☐Jesus used two verses from the Old Testament to give His summary of the whole law. Look up and read Deuteronomy 6:5 and Leviticus 19:18.
☐Add a third picture to your Picture Poster. Have each child draw a heart as a symbol of the two greatest commandments to love God and to love each other.

PRAYER
Father in Heaven,
There is so much we do not understand. Help us to learn how to really listen to You as You speak to us through Your Word and in our hearts as we pray to You. We want to love You with all our heart, soul, and mind. We want to love our friends and family—but we fall far short. Teach us how to love the way You love us. In the name of Jesus. Amen.

THE ANOINTING OF JESUS

OPENING THOUGHTS

☐ If you had unlimited resources, what would you do to show your affection to someone you love?

☐ As the final events of His life on earth unfolded, Jesus was keenly aware of His impending death. In a beautiful display of devotion Mary anointed Jesus one evening in Bethany. Only later did she really understand the significance of what she had done.

MARK 14:3-11

While [Jesus] was in Bethany, reclining at the table in the home of a man known as Simon the Leper, a woman came with an alabaster jar of very expensive perfume, made of pure nard. She broke the jar and poured the perfume on his head.

Some of those present were saying indignantly to one another, "Why this waste of perfume? It could have been sold for more than a year's wages and the money given to the poor." And they rebuked her harshly.

"Leave her alone," said Jesus. "Why are you bothering her? She has done a beautiful thing to me. The poor you will always have with you, and you can help them any time you want. But you will not always have me. She did what she could. She poured perfume on my body beforehand to prepare for my burial. I tell you the truth, wherever the gospel is preached throughout the world, what she has done will also be told, in memory of her."

DISCUSSION AND REFLECTION

1. How did Jesus react to the criticism the woman received for being extravagant?
2. What are some of the ways that you try to show your devotion to Jesus?
3. "Each man should give what he has decided in his heart to give, not reluctantly or under compulsion, for God loves a cheerful giver" (2 Corinthians 9:7). When you give your time and resources to God do you have this attitude? Why, or why not?

FAMILY ACTIVITIES

☐ Think of something you can do as a display of affection to the Lord. Each family member may want to do something on his own or you may decide to do something as a family. See how many ideas you can come up with, then choose between your options. Here are a few suggestions to get you started:

1. Give up a favorite television show this week. Spend the time reading the Bible, or a book that will encourage you in your walk with the Lord.
2. Bake a batch of cookies. Take some to a friend or neighbor who needs encouragement.
3. Think of something you have that you could give to someone in need. Then do it.
4. Write out a prayer to God expressing your feelings.
5. Make a commitment to spend time alone in prayer and Bible reading *every* day for the next week.
6. Make a commitment to follow through with what God is asking you to change in your life.
7. Start a spiritual journal where you record your thoughts and prayers on a regular basis.
8. Invite some neighbors over for dinner, and share with them one thing the Lord has done for you.
9. Do a simple fast. For example, give up desserts for two days, or don't eat any snacks after dinner for several days. When you are tempted to eat focus your thoughts on the Lord and His love. Ask Him to help you walk more closely with Him.

☐ Complete the fourth box in your Picture Poster. Have each child draw a perfume bottle to remember the extravagant gift of devotion given to Jesus.

PRAYER

Dear Lord Jesus,

Help us to be like Mary. May we too respond to You with acts of devotion. Like Mary, may our acts of devotion be unhindered by worries of what other people will think. Help us to follow through with the leadings of Your Spirit even when we do not fully understand what You are asking us to do. Amen.

THURSDAY—THE LAST SUPPER

THE FAREWELL FEAST

THURSDAY'S SCRIPTURE

OPENING THOUGHTS

☐ Imagine that tonight was the last dinner you would ever have here on earth with your family. How would you feel?

☐ This day is sometimes called Maundy Thursday, from the Latin word for mandate or command. During their last meal together, Jesus gave His disciples the command to love each other as He had loved them.

JOHN 13:1-5,12-17,34

It was just before the Passover Feast. Jesus knew that the time had come for him to leave this world and go to the Father. Having loved his own who were in the world, he now showed them the full extent of his love.

The evening meal was being served, and the devil had already prompted Judas Iscariot, son of Simon, to betray Jesus. Jesus knew that the Father had put all things under his power, and that he had come from God and was returning to God; so he got up from the meal, took off his outer clothing, and wrapped a towel around his waist. After that, he poured water into a basin and began to wash his disciples' feet, drying them with the towel that was wrapped around him. . . .

When he had finished washing their feet, he put on his clothes and returned to his place. "Do you understand what I have done for you?" he asked them. "You call me 'Teacher' and 'Lord,' and rightly so, for that is what I am. Now that I, your Lord and Teacher, have washed your feet, you also should wash one another's feet. I have set you an example that you should do as I have done for you. I tell you the truth, no servant is greater than his master, nor is a messenger greater than the one who sent him. Now that you know these things, you will be blessed if you do them. . . .

"A new command I give you: Love one another. As I have loved you, so you must love one another."

MATTHEW 26:26-30

While they were eating, Jesus took bread, gave thanks and broke it, and gave it to his disciples, saying, "Take and eat; this is my body."

Then he took the cup, gave thanks and offered it to them, saying, "Drink from it, all of you. This is my blood of the covenant, which is poured out for many for the forgiveness of sins. I tell you, I will not drink of this fruit of the vine from now on until that day when I drink it anew with you in my Father's kingdom."

When they had sung a hymn, they went out to the Mount of Olives.

FAIREST LORD JESUS

Fairest Lord Jesus, Ruler of all nature,
O Thou of God and man the Son:
Thee will I cherish, Thee will I honor,
Thou my soul's glory, joy, and crown.

Fair are the meadows, Fairer still the woodlands,
Robed in the blooming garb of spring:
Jesus is fairer, Jesus is purer,
Who makes the woeful heart to sing.

Fair is the sunshine, Fairer still the moonlight,
And all the twinkling starry host:
Jesus shines brighter, Jesus shines purer
Than all the angels heaven can boast.

Beautiful Savior! Lord of the nations!
Son of God and Son of Man!
Glory and honor, Praise, adoration,
Now and forevermore be Thine!

From Münster Gesangbuch, *Anonymous*
Crusaders' Hymn, Silesian Folk Melody

JONI EARECKSON TADA is the founder and president of Joni and Friends. The ministry of this organization includes an information and referral program, workshops, audio-visual materials, and the Christian Fund for the Disabled, a financial assistance program. She serves on the National Council on Disability to which she was appointed by President Reagan in 1987.

In 1967, Joni broke her neck in a diving accident, which left her paralyzed from the shoulders down. Joni told the story in her best-selling autobiography *Joni*. In response to thousands who wrote concerning their own problems with pain and suffering, Joni wrote her second book *A Step Further*. Her other books include *Choices . . . Changes, Secret Strength,* and *Glorious Intruder*.

Joni's inspirational radio program is heard daily on over 500 stations by millions of listeners.

Jesus' Pre-Cross Crash Course

BY JONI EARECKSON TADA

ave you ever crammed for a "this-is-it, now-or-never" Bible exam? Studied for a crash course on systematic theology? Unless you're a seminary student working on your Doctorate, probably not. But suppose you were suddenly and unexpectedly thrust into such a situation? Would you panic? You bet!

That's probably how the disciples felt the Thursday night after the Last Supper. Up until that point, the evening had been quiet, intimate, warm, and personal. They had enjoyed the Passover feast together, and then there was that touching moment when Jesus washed their feet, leaving them an example of love and humility.

But then the mood shifted slightly. There were those strange words the Lord spoke to Judas, "What you are about to do, do quickly." Judas suddenly left and, from that point on, the tone of the evening somehow changed. It was still intimate and personal, but a sense of urgency, a strange passion filled the room. It was as if the Lord realized He had many pressing things to say, and only a short time in which to say them.

He told them He was going away, but explained that they couldn't follow Him. He spoke about His relationship with the Father. He talked about the continuing intimacy He would share with His followers, using the analogy of a vine and its branches—Jesus said that He would be closely linked to them, even after He departed.

THURSDAY / THE FAREWELL FEAST

He talked of persecution. He spoke about peace. He talked about people who would believe and others who would doubt. He talked of grief and comfort. He foretold the future. He promised His return. And then the disciples marveled as their Lord prayed a heart-wrenching prayer.

The disciples' heads must have been spinning!

So much was jammed-packed into those few short hours. Jesus had so much to teach in each discourse, encouragement, prediction, and commandment. There was so little time to say everything that was so necessary to the life of these disciples, men who would make up the foundation of His world-wide Church.

If the hours weren't short enough, the evening was dramatically cut short by the Roman soldiers and Pharisees who came to arrest the Lord. Perhaps the disciples found themselves thinking or even saying, "Wait, not now! There's so much You've said . . . life and death issues . . . so much that we don't understand, that we can't remember. We can't contain it all!"

Yet Jesus knew the unspoken cries of their hearts. And He knew His disciples would face even more questions as the events of the following days would unfurl. The disciples would become even more confused. But Jesus also knew . . . everything would become clear.

That's why He promised them the Holy Spirit who would unravel everything. The Comforter would guide and direct each disciple. The Lord even added, "I have much more to say to you, more than you can now bear. But when He, the Spirit of truth, comes, He will guide you into all truth. . . . He will bring glory to Me by taking from what is Mine and making it known to you."

Perhaps it was a kind of risk on the part of Christ to entrust so much precious and priceless spiritual truth into the hands of a bunch of bewildered men. But Jesus knew those men far better than they knew themselves. The Spirit would gently remind them. He would make things abundantly clear.

Are we any different than the disciples? Not really. There are times when we must feel like God is trying to pour million-gallon truths into our one-ounce brains. There are times when, perusing the Bible, we must marvel at how one could possibly comprehend it all, take it all in. If the disciples were bewildered and perplexed, where does that put us—feeble, finite, and frail people that we are?

But Jesus knows it all. He knows us. He knows that, by His Holy Spirit and with time, it will all be made clear.

DISCUSSION AND REFLECTION

1. What truths in Scripture are especially puzzling to you? Each person should name at least one specific area. Then decide which subject you might want to study as a family in the near future.
2. In what ways could you allow the Holy Spirit, who is the Counselor and Comforter, to teach you?
3. During the Last Supper, Jesus demonstrated a beautiful example of service to His disciples when He washed their feet. What ways do you serve each other as a family? What *new* ways can you think of to serve each other better?

ADDITIONAL READING

PASSOVER: A PORTRAIT OF CHRIST
By Stan Kellner

G rowing up in a Jewish family and celebrating the Passover since I was four years old should have given me a complete understanding of the meaning of this important religious holiday. As the youngest in the family it was customary that I ask the question (in

Hebrew), "Why is this night different from all other nights?" As a part of the ceremony my question received four different answers. But it wasn't until years later when I became a Christian that I came to understand the full meaning of Passover.

When Jews celebrate Passover, they focus on what God did for the Israelites when He delivered them from the bondage of slavery. (See Exodus 12.) The basic elements of the Passover meal have not changed to this day. Three of the central elements are the lamb shankbone, the Matzo (unleavened bread), and the four cups of wine. But for many Jews they have little meaning. There is no life in the ceremony. As a Christian, I came to realize that the Passover is filled with spiritual symbolism.

The lamb shankbone, which represents the sacrifice of an innocent unblemished lamb, points directly to Jesus. So also, Jesus was perfect, without sin, "the Lamb of God, who takes away the sin of the world" (John 1:29).

The Matzo, unleavened bread, portrays the sinless Christ beautifully. Leaven is often used as a symbol for sin. Jesus said, "I am the bread of life. He who comes to me will never go hungry, and he who believes in me will never be thirsty" (John 6:35). Jesus is our unleavened bread.

A piece of Matzo has holes through it to prevent any rising, marks from the roasting process that look almost like bruises, and stripes on it from the grate it was cooked on. Likewise, Jesus "was wounded for our transgressions, he was bruised for our iniquities . . . and with his stripes we are healed" (Isaiah 53:5, KJV).

During the Passover, four cups of wine are consumed, each symbolizing a specific working of God to deliver Israel. The third cup is the "cup of redemption," possibly the very cup Jesus used with bread in His Last Supper with the disciples to institute what we refer to as the Lord's Supper. He also used that cup to prophesy His impending death, which would bring redemption and forgiveness of sin to mankind.

As I began to see this incredible symbolism, my understanding of the Passover was changed forever. How fitting that God chose the day of Passover for the death of Jesus.

For you know that it was not with perishable things such as silver or gold that you were redeemed from the empty way of life handed down to you from your forefathers, but with the precious blood of Christ, a lamb without blemish or defect. (1 Peter 1:18-19)

Stan and his wife, Nita, are field missionaries with International Students Incorporated (ISI) serving in Colorado Springs. For the past twelve years Stan has been leading groups through a "Christ and the Passover" presentation.

MATTHEW 26:36-46

Then Jesus went with his disciples to a place called Gethsemane, and he said to them, "Sit here while I go over there and pray." He took Peter and the two sons of Zebedee along with him, and he began to be sorrowful and troubled.

Then he said to them, "My soul is overwhelmed with sorrow to the point of death. Stay here and keep watch with me."

Going a little farther, he fell with his face to the ground and prayed, "My Father, if it is possible, may this cup be taken from me. Yet not as I will, but as you will."

Then he returned to his disciples and found them sleeping. "Could you men not keep watch with me for one hour?" he asked Peter. "Watch and pray so that you will not fall into temptation. The spirit is willing, but the body is weak."

He went away a second time and prayed, "My Father, if it is not possible for this cup to be taken away unless I drink it, may your will be done."

When he came back, he again found them sleeping, because their eyes were heavy. So he left them and went away once more and prayed the third time, saying the same thing.

Then he returned to the disciples and said to them, "Are you still sleeping and resting? Look, the hour is near, and the Son of Man is betrayed into the hands of sinners. Rise, let us go! Here comes my betrayer!"

FAMILY ACTIVITIES

Focus on servanthood. Before you eat your dinner tonight, have the father or another adult use a wet washcloth to wash the hands of each person at the table. How does it feel having someone else do for you what you should have done yourself before coming to the table?

☐ ☐ ☐

An exercise in being alone. You will need:
☐ Piece of paper for each person
☐ Pencil or pen for each person

Read the account of Jesus and His disciples in the Garden of Gethsemane. (See "Additional Reading," Matthew 26:36-46.) Take a few minutes for each family member to be alone. Small children may simply go to a corner of the same room as an adult. Focus for a few minutes on how Jesus must have felt in the Garden. His friends had fallen asleep. Unable to persevere in prayer, they left Him alone with incomprehensible spiritual agony.

Jesus knew what lay ahead, and He had to face it alone. Nothing we experience can even come close to what Jesus endured in the Garden, but all of us feel alone at times.

Think about the times when you feel alone and misunderstood. How can thinking about what Jesus went through on your behalf help you when you feel alone? Write down your thoughts in the form of a prayer. When everyone in your family is reunited, share your thoughts with each other.

□ □ □

Attend a worship service and receive communion. It was at the Last Supper that Jesus instituted communion. For this reason some churches serve communion on Maundy Thursday. If your church does not have such a service, visit a church that does. This might be a chance to see how a church different from your own worships God.

□ □ □

Add a fifth picture to your Poster. Have the children draw a simple picture of the bread and the cup from the Last Supper.

PASSOVER LAMB

It is truly right and good, always and everywhere,
  with our whole heart and mind and voice,
to praise you, the invisible, almighty, and eternal God,
  and your only-begotten Son, Jesus Christ our Lord;
for he is the true Paschal Lamb,
  who at the feast of the Passover
paid for us the debt of Adam's sin,
  and by his blood delivered your faithful people.

This is the night, when you brought our fathers,
  the children of Israel, out of bondage in Egypt,
and led them through the Red Sea on dry land. . . .

How wonderful and beyond our knowing, O God,
  is your mercy and loving-kindness to us,
that to redeem a slave, you gave a Son.

How holy is this night, when wickedness is put to flight,
  and sin is washed away.
It restores innocence to the fallen,
  and joy to those who mourn.
It casts out pride and hatred, and brings peace and concord.

How blessed is this night,
  when earth and heaven are joined
and man is reconciled to God.

From the Book of Common Prayer

P R A Y E R

Father,
We have many unanswered questions. What a comfort to know that someday we will sit at Jesus' feet and have one great long Bible study to end all Bible studies! Thank You for the Holy Spirit who teaches us gently here and now. Give us teachable spirits so that we can learn from Him. In Jesus' name. Amen.

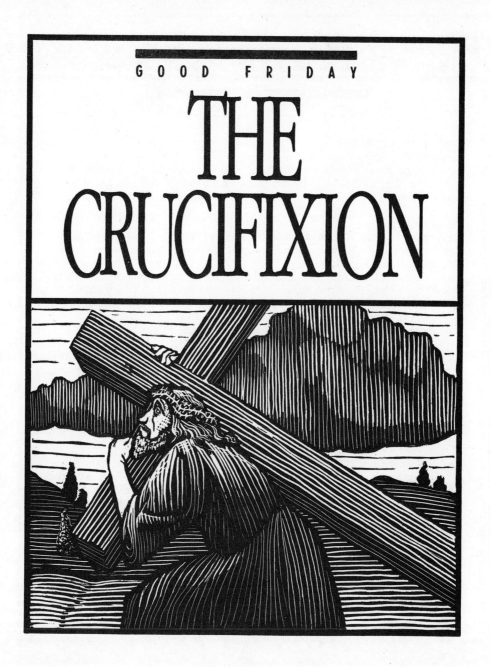

GOOD FRIDAY'S SCRIPTURE

OPENING THOUGHTS
☐ Why do you think this day is called "good"?
☐ In Scripture the place where the Crucifixion took place is called Golgotha, which means the place of the skull. *Calvary* is the Latin word for skull, Golgotha is the Aramaic word.

JOHN 19:17-30
Carrying his own cross, [Jesus] went out to the place of the skull (which in Aramaic is called Golgotha). Here they crucified him, and with him two others—one on each side and Jesus in the middle.

Pilate had a notice prepared and fastened to the cross. It read: JESUS OF NAZARETH, THE KING OF THE JEWS. Many of the Jews read this sign, for the place where Jesus was crucified was near the city, and the sign was written in Aramaic, Latin and Greek. The chief priests of the Jews protested to Pilate, "Do not write 'The King of the Jews,' but that this man claimed to be king of the Jews."

Pilate answered, "What I have written, I have written."

When the soldiers crucified Jesus, they took his clothes, dividing them into four shares, one for each of them, with the undergarment remaining. This garment was seamless, woven in one piece from top to bottom.

"Let's not tear it," they said to one another. "Let's decide by lot who will get it."

This happened that the scripture might be fulfilled which said,

"They divided my garments among them
   and cast lots for my clothing."

So this is what the soldiers did.

Near the cross of Jesus stood his mother, his mother's sister, Mary the wife of Clopas, and Mary Magdalene. When Jesus saw his mother there, and the disciple whom he loved standing nearby, he said to his mother, "Dear woman, here is your son," and to the disciple, "Here is your mother." From that time on, this disciple took her into his home.

Later, knowing that all was now completed, and so that the Scripture would be fulfilled, Jesus said, "I am thirsty." A jar of wine vinegar was there, so they soaked a sponge in it, put the sponge on a stalk of the hyssop plant, and lifted it to Jesus' lips. When he had received the drink, Jesus said, "It is finished." With that, he bowed his head and gave up his spirit.

WHEN I SURVEY THE WONDROUS CROSS

When I survey the wondrous cross
On which the Prince of glory died,
My richest gain I count but loss,
And pour contempt on all my pride.

Forbid it, Lord, that I should boast,
Save in the death of Christ, my God;
All the vain things that charm me most,
I sacrifice them to His blood.

See, from His head, His hands, His feet,
Sorrow and love flow mingled down:
Did e'er such love and sorrow meet,
Or thorns compose so rich a crown?

Were the whole realm of nature mine,
That were a present far too small;
Love so amazing, so divine,
Demands my soul, my life, my all.

Isaac Watts, 1674-1748, Author
Based on a Gregorian chant
Arranged by Lowell Mason, 1792-1872

CHARLES COLSON received his bachelor's degree from Brown University and his law degree from George Washington University. From 1969–1973 he served as special counsel to President Richard M. Nixon. He pleaded guilty to charges related to Watergate in 1974 and served seven months in prison. He is now chairman of Prison Fellowship Ministries, a Washington, D.C.-based organization that he founded in 1976.

Colson is the author of several books including *Born Again, Loving God, Kingdoms in Conflict,* and *Against the Night.* All of his speaking fees and book royalties are donated to further the work of Prison Fellowship Ministries, P. O. Box 17500, Washington, DC 20041, (703) 478-0100.

The Innocent Prisoner

BY CHARLES COLSON

he prisoner said nothing as people shouted charges against him. He had been pushed from place to place and questioned throughout the long night. His body hurt as he stood before his accusers.

He knew what it was to be alone. One of his friends had become a snitch and turned him in. Now he stood before the governor, the man who could set him free with one stroke of his pen.

The governor sighed. He could see that the man was innocent. He offered the prisoner a chance to plea bargain, but the man would not lie in order to save himself. "What have you done?" the governor demanded.

The prisoner looked steadily at the governor. "I was born and now live, to bear witness to the truth," he said. The governor shook his head. "Truth," he said tiredly. "What is truth?"

He turned to the angry crowd pressing against the gates. "Release another prisoner, but not this man! Execute him!" they cried. They screamed until their voices gave out. They were like a pack of dogs barking for fresh blood.

The governor shrugged. The mob grew quiet as the governor stood to speak. "I personally find this man not guilty," he said. "He has committed no crime, and certainly doesn't deserve the death penalty. But he's your business, not mine. By the power vested in me, I sentence him to death—today." The air was still for a moment, then filled with cheers. The governor's public image was safe.

The guards led the prisoner away. They ripped off his clothes, and beat him with a nail-studded whip until his back was a mass of bloody flesh. Then they took him to a hilltop outside of town at a well-traveled crossroads. They laid the prisoner on a rough wooden cross. Blood flowed from his wrists and ankles as the guards pounded spikes through his flesh into the hard wood. Onlookers jeered as the cross was lifted into the air. It stood dark and ugly against the morning sky.

Two convicted thieves hung on either side of him. One angrily cursed, "Aren't you the Christ? Save yourself and us!"

The other criminal rebuked him: "Don't you fear God? We were condemned fairly—we are guilty. But this man has done nothing wrong." He actually believed that this man hanging next to him could forgive his sins. He cried out, "Remember me when you come into your kingdom!"

The prisoner turned toward him, "Today you will be with me in Heaven."

The blood continued to flow from his ragged wounds; his breathing grew labored, then shallow, then stopped. After three hours of agony, with a loud cry, the ordeal was over—he was dead.

What Jesus endured on the cross is beyond our comprehension. He bore the punishment for all the sins of the world, for all time. He carried the full load of God's wrath against sin. He went through spiritual agony beyond anything mortal man is capable of experiencing. The God-man did for us what we could never do for ourselves.

But this horrible execution was not the end. Jesus was condemned and killed for claiming he was God. He proved his claims were true when three days later he rose from the dead.

Yes, Jesus Christ, the innocent prisoner, still lives today. That fact gives hope and meaning to every person. We all stand condemned before God. We have all fallen short of what God wants for us. What God requires of us is perfect righteousness. Through faith in Jesus, God considers Jesus' righteousness as ours.

God's desire is to have a personal relationship with each of us. He wants to know us—and he wants us to know him. Jesus' death made this possible.

Jesus' love is real. His love is tough enough to give everything. He died as a prisoner in order to overcome death for the rest of us. He became like us so that we could become like him—righteous before God.

You can be like that thief next to Jesus, who complained angrily to God, and rejected Jesus. Or you can be like the other thief, recognizing Jesus for who he is—the holy Son of God. The choice is yours.

DISCUSSION AND REFLECTION

1. In what way were you actually there at Calvary with Jesus?
2. Why was Jesus' suffering so much worse than what anyone else has ever suffered?
3. Perhaps you have heard the story of the Crucifixion many times. What thoughts or feelings did you have this time when you heard the story?

ISAIAH 53:4-6

Surely he took up our infirmities
    and carried our sorrows,
yet we considered him stricken by God,
    smitten by him, and afflicted.
But he was pierced for our transgressions,
    he was crushed for our iniquities;
the punishment that brought us peace was upon him,
    and by his wounds we are healed.
We all, like sheep, have gone astray,
    each of us has turned to his own way;
and the LORD has laid on him
    the iniquity of us all.

The center of salvation is the Cross of Jesus, and the reason it is so easy to obtain salvation is because it cost God so much. The cross is the point where God and sinful man merge with a crash and the way to life is opened—but the crash is on the heart of God.

Oswald Chambers, My Utmost For His Highest

The essence of sin is man substituting himself for God, while the essence of salvation is God substituting himself for man.

John R. W. Stott, The Cross of Christ

THE LIVING WORD

Corrie ten Boom was arrested, along with the rest of her family, for harboring Jews in Holland during World War II. This short passage from her book The Hiding Place *takes place in the Ravensbruck concentration camp in Germany. Corrie's sister, Betsie, had just read, "In all these things we are more than conquerors through him who loved us" (Romans 8:37).*

I would look about us as Betsie read, watching the light leap from face to face. More than conquerors. . . . It was not a wish. It was a fact. We knew it, we experienced it minute by minute—poor, hated, hungry. We are more than conquerors. Not "we shall be." We are! Life in Ravensbruck took place on two separate levels, mutually impossible. One, the observable, external life, grew every day more horrible. The other, the life we lived with God, grew daily better, truth upon truth, glory upon glory.

    Sometimes I would slip the Bible from its little sack with hands that shook, so mysterious had it become to me. It was new; it had just been written. I marveled sometimes that the ink was dry. I had believed the Bible always, but reading it now had nothing to do with belief. It was simply a description of the way things were—of hell and heaven, of how men act and how God acts. I had read a thousand times the story of Jesus' arrest—how soldiers had slapped Him, laughed at Him, flogged Him. Now such happenings had faces and voices.

Taken from The Hiding Place *by Corrie ten Boom with John and Elizabeth Sherrill (Chosen Books Inc., Chappaqua, New York). Corrie (1892-1983) lived in Holland with her family and worked as a watchmaker until the ten Booms were arrested for hiding Jews during World War II. She was released from Ravensbruck in 1945. Corrie spent the next thirty-three years traveling all over the world captivating audiences with her story of God's grace in the midst of her imprisonment. Her inspiring books include* In My Father's House *and* Tramp for the Lord.

ROCK OF AGES

Rock of Ages, cleft for me,
Let me hide myself in Thee!
Let the water and the blood
From Thy riven side which flow'd,
Be of sin the double cure,
Cleanse me from its guilt and power.

Not the labors of my hands
Can fulfil Thy law's demands;
Could my zeal no respite know,
Could my tears for ever flow,
All for sin could not atone;
Thou must save, and Thou alone.

Nothing in my hand I bring;
Simply to Thy Cross I cling;
Naked, come to Thee for dress;
Helpless, look to Thee for grace;
Foul, I to the Fountain fly;
Wash me, Saviour, or I die!

Augustus Montague Toplady, 1740-1778

THE CROSS

By A. W. Tozer

To go along with Christ step by step and point by point in identical suffering of Roman crucifixion is not possible for any of us, and certainly is not intended by our Lord.
An earnest Christian woman long ago sought help from Henry Suso concerning her

spiritual life. She had been imposing austerities upon herself in an effort to feel the sufferings that Christ had felt on the cross. Things were not going so well with her and Suso knew why.

The old saint wrote his spiritual daughter and reminded her that our Lord had not said, "If any man will come after me, let him deny himself, and take up MY cross." He had said, "Let him . . . take up his cross." There is a difference of only one small pronoun; but that difference is vast and important.

Crosses are all alike, but no two are identical. Never before nor since has there been a cross experience just like that endured by the Saviour. The whole dreadful work of dying which Christ suffered was something unique in the experience of mankind. It had to be so if the cross was to mean life for the world. The sin-bearing, the darkness, the rejection by the Father were agonies peculiar to the Person of the holy sacrifice. For anyone to claim that experience of Christ would be sacrilege.

Every cross was and is an instrument of death, but no man could die on the cross of another; hence Jesus said, "Let him . . . take up his cross, and follow me!"

Reprinted from "The Cross You Bear Is Yours—Not Christ's," Renewed Day by Day. Used by permission of Christian Publications. A. W. Tozer (1897-1963) was pastor of Southside Alliance Church in Chicago for thirty-one years. Called "a twentieth-century prophet," he wrote thirty-four books, including The Pursuit of God, The Divine Conquest, *and* The Knowledge of the Holy.

FAMILY ACTIVITIES

Dramatize the fact that *our* sins put Jesus on the cross. You will need:
- ☐ Large nail for each person
- ☐ Piece of wood, at least 2″ x 4″ in dimension
- ☐ Hammer

Have your family sit on the floor together, facing each other. Place the piece of wood in the middle. Give each person a nail to hold.

For a short time, each family member should reflect silently on his own sins. Think of recent things you have thought, said, or done that were not pleasing to the Lord.

If anyone present has never accepted Jesus as his Savior, asking Him for forgiveness and new life, this would be a perfect opportunity to make that commitment. (Have that person pray a prayer like this one: Lord Jesus, Please forgive me for my sins. I believe that You died for me. I accept You as my Lord and Savior. Come into my heart and into my life. I want to live my life for You. Amen.)

After a few minutes of silence each person should hammer his nail into the wood. Younger children will need help.

Read aloud the following verse:

1 PETER 2:24

[Jesus] himself bore our sins in his body on the tree, so that we might die to sins and live for righteousness; by his wounds you have been healed.

Join hands for a closing prayer, expressing thoughts like these: Precious Jesus, We are humbled as we realize that *our* sins nailed You to the cross. You purchased our forgiveness with Your own blood. Help us to walk more fully in the new life of righteousness that You purchased for us at such a great cost. It is in Your name that we pray. Amen.

□ □ □

Dramatize the fact that our sins once confessed and turned from are completely forgiven. You will need:

☐Paper for each person
☐Pencil or pen for each person

1. Each person should reflect on his failure to live a life that is pleasing to God. Make a list of the things for which you need to be forgiven.
2. Have each person pray aloud or silently, asking God for forgiveness. If you have a fireplace, throw each person's paper into it and burn them. If you don't have a fireplace, crumple up the lists and throw them in the trash.
3. Close this time of seeking forgiveness by reading the following verse:

1 JOHN 1:9

If we confess our sins, he is faithful and just and will forgive us our sins and purify us from all unrighteousness.

□ □ □

Ask each child to draw a small picture of a cross to place in the sixth box in your Picture Poster.

A PRAYER OF REFLECTION ON THE LAST WORDS OF CHRIST

We have a fascination with the final words of the dying. With Jesus' last words we are not disappointed. Resounding through the ages in the Word of God, they stand perfect and complete. As we focus on those words, we look for a window to eternity, and in the process find a spotlight on our own soul.

"Father, forgive them, for they do not know what they are doing" (Luke 23:34).
Lord, I hold on to a grudge like it was a treasure, but it rots my soul. Help me to let go of what I can't control and learn to forgive.

"I tell you the truth, today you will be with me in paradise" (Luke 23:43).
Like the thief to whom You promised eternal life, I believe in Your ability to save me. Help my unbelief.

"He said to his mother, 'Dear woman, here is your son,' and to his disciple, 'Here is your mother'" (John 19:26-27).
When I hurt, I think only of myself. Give me an unselfish heart to see and care for others who are hurting.

"My God, my God, why have you forsaken me?" (Matthew 27:46).
It was for me that You were forsaken. Help me to let go of the unanswered "whys?" in my life and to find peace in knowing that You are my God.

"I am thirsty" (John 19:28).
Give me an unquenchable thirst to know You, my Lord.

"It is finished" (John 19:30).
I can never add to what you have done for me. My salvation is complete. Help me to know the joy of Your grace as I serve You.

"Father, into your hands I commit my spirit" (Luke 23:46).
I want to surrender everything in my life to You. Teach me what that means for each new day, and give me the will to do what I know I need to do. Amen.

PRAYER

Precious Savior,
The extent of Your love over-
whelms us. Help us to take our
sins seriously, and to always
remember the high price You paid
in taking the punishment we
deserve for those sins. Thank You,
Lord, for dying on the Cross for us.
Amen.

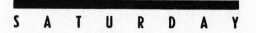

SATURDAY

IN THE TOMB

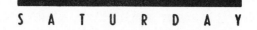

IN THE TOMB

OPENING THOUGHTS
☐ Has anyone close to you ever died? If so, how did you feel right after that person died?
☐ The guard at the tomb probably consisted of four Roman soldiers. The punishment for a Roman soldier who deserted his post was death. The seal was probably a cord stretched across the stone at the entrance to the tomb and attached to each side.

MATTHEW 12:39-41
He answered, "A wicked and adulterous generation asks for a miraculous sign! But none will be given it except the sign of the prophet Jonah. For as Jonah was three days and three nights in the belly of a huge fish, so the Son of Man will be three days and three nights in the heart of the earth. The men of Nineveh will stand up at the judgment with this generation and condemn it; for they repented at the preaching of Jonah, and now one greater than Jonah is here.

MATTHEW 27:62-66
The next day, the one after Preparation Day, the chief priests and the Pharisees went to Pilate. "Sir," they said, "we remember that while he was still alive that deceiver said, 'After three days I will rise again.' So give the order for the tomb to be made secure until the third day. Otherwise, his disciples may come and steal the body and tell the people that he has been raised from the dead. This last deception will be worse than the first."

"Take a guard," Pilate answered. "Go, make the tomb as secure as you know how." So they went and made the tomb secure by putting a seal on the stone and posting the guard.

DISCUSSION AND REFLECTION
1. Why did the chief priests and the Pharisees request a guard and a seal on the tomb? What did their request actually accomplish?
2. The disciples were discouraged and confused as they gathered after Jesus' death (John 20:9,19). It seems that they did not really expect Jesus to rise from the dead as He had promised. Perhaps you are in a time of difficulty and waiting in your life. Are there things you need to trust God for? Are there truths He has made clear to you that you are still not really believing?

FAMILY ACTIVITIES
☐ Read the story of Jonah in a Bible storybook or in the Bible (Jonah 1–4).
☐ Add a seventh picture to your Poster. Have each child draw the big rock that was placed in front of the tomb.

PRAYER
Gracious Lord,
Thank You for Your Word, the Bible. Help us to listen to what You are saying to us through Your Word. Help us to believe what You have said and to act upon it in our lives. In Jesus' name. Amen.

EASTER SUNDAY

THE RESURRECTION

EASTER SUNDAY'S SCRIPTURE

OPENING THOUGHTS

☐ Why do you think there is more tradition and celebration associated with Christmas than with Easter?

☐ In the early Church on Easter Day, Christians greeted each other with the words, "He is risen!" The response was, "He is risen indeed!" Greet a friend that way today.

JOHN 20:1-18

Early on the first day of the week, while it was still dark, Mary Magdalene went to the tomb and saw that the stone had been removed from the entrance. So she came running to Simon Peter and the other disciple, the one Jesus loved, and said, "They have taken the Lord out of the tomb, and we don't know where they have put him!"

So Peter and the other disciple started for the tomb. Both were running, but the other disciple outran Peter and reached the tomb first. He bent over and looked in at the strips of linen lying there but did not go in. Then Simon Peter, who was behind him, arrived and went into the tomb. He saw the strips of linen lying there, as well as the burial cloth that had been around Jesus' head. The cloth was folded up by itself, separate from the linen. Finally the other disciple, who had reached the tomb first, also went inside. He saw and believed. (They still did not understand from Scripture that Jesus had to rise from the dead.)

Then the disciples went back to their homes, but Mary stood outside the tomb crying. As she wept, she bent over to look into the tomb and saw two angels in white, seated where Jesus' body had been, one at the head and the other at the foot.

They asked her, "Woman, why are you crying?"

"They have taken my Lord away," she said, "and I don't know where they have put him." At this, she turned around and saw Jesus standing there, but she did not realize that it was Jesus.

"Woman," he said, "why are you crying? Who is it you are looking for?"

Thinking he was the gardener, she said, "Sir, if you have carried him away, tell me where you have put him, and I will get him."

Jesus said to her, "Mary."

She turned toward him and cried out in Aramaic, "Rabboni!" (which means Teacher).

Jesus said, "Do not hold on to me, for I have not yet returned to the Father. Go instead to my brothers and tell them, 'I am returning to my Father and your Father, to my God and your God.' "

Mary Magdalene went to the disciples with the news: "I have seen the Lord!" And she told them that he had said these things to her.

CHRIST THE LORD IS RISEN TODAY

Christ the Lord is risen today, Alleluia!
Sons of men and angels say: Alleluia!
Raise your joys and triumphs high, Alleluia!
Sing, ye heavens, and earth reply: Alleluia!

Lives again our glorious King, Alleluia!
Where, O death, is now thy sting? Alleluia!
Dying once, he all doth save, Alleluia!
Where thy victory, O grave? Alleluia!

Love's redeeming work is done, Alleluia!
Fought the fight, the battle won, Alleluia!
Death in vain forbids him rise, Alleluia!
Christ has opened Paradise, Alleluia!

Soar we now where Christ has led, Alleluia!
Following our exalted Head, Alleluia!
Made like him, like him we rise, Alleluia!
Ours the cross, the grave, the skies, Alleluia!

Hail the Lord of earth and heaven! Alleluia!
Praise to thee by both be given, Alleluia!
Thee we greet triumphant now, Alleluia!
Hail, the Resurrection thou! Alleluia!

Charles Wesley, 1707-1788, Author
Arrangement from "Lyra Davidica," 1708

BILLY GRAHAM is the founder of the Billy Graham Evangelistic Association and has had a worldwide ministry since his 1949 Los Angeles Crusade vaulted him into the public's eye. Originally scheduled for three weeks, the event continued for more than two months, with overflow crowds filling the huge tent each night. Since that time he has preached to more than 100 million people in every state in the United States and eighty-four foreign countries.

Billy Graham has received a wide range of awards and honorary doctorates from institutions in this country and abroad. His weekly radio program "Hour of Decision" is broadcast by more than 500 stations around the world. Billy Graham has written fifteen books including *How to Be Born Again, Facing Death and the Life After,* and *Answers to Life's Problems.*

EASTER SUNDAY / THE RESURRECTION

We Too Shall Live

BY BILLY GRAHAM

here are far more pretentious burial places than the grave where the lifeless body of the Savior was laid two thousand years ago. In Egypt may be found the resting places of the great pharaohs, buried in lavish wealth in tombs of artistic design. The Taj Mahal in India is probably the most dazzling of all tombs. The grave of the prophet Mohammed is guarded in Medina and visited by devoted Muslims. In Moscow's Red Square lies the crystal casket of Lenin, which has been viewed by millions. But the exact site of the grave of Jesus Christ is not definitely known and cannot be authenticated.

While other tombs are evidence of death and decay, Christ's tomb alone is the evidence of life. Today we hear again the challenge of the angel in the garden, "Why do you seek the living among the dead?"

Even though there are scoffers who still demand, "Where is the proof of the next life? Where is the evidence of the Resurrection?" to us Christians the Resurrection, the empty tomb, is the very heart of our faith. Without it we have nothing.

Historians accept as fact past occurrences for which they can produce only shreds of evidence. But the Resurrection was attested to by hundreds of New Testament witnesses who saw Jesus Christ, talked with Him, ate with Him, walked with Him, knelt before Him, and acclaimed Him as their Lord and Savior. If the statements of those who testified to the truth of the Resurrection are not accepted as conclusive evidence, then no testimony and no evidence whatever can establish any truth in any age of history.

What was it that took the first company of disciples, cowering as they did behind locked doors, and transformed them into a band of champions of their crucified Lord? It could never have been a dead leader. It had to be a living, conquering Christ. What power and influence changed the cross from an instrument of bloody torture into the most glorious and beloved of all symbols? The Romans had crucified thousands of people before and after Calvary. If Jesus had not risen from the dead, no right-minded person would have glorified anything so hideous and repulsive as a cross.

What gave the great army of Christian martyrs and missionaries the love and power to face death, penetrate poisonous jungles, cross deserts, and hasten to the ends of the earth in their zeal to win disciples to Christ? It was the eternal fact of the Resurrection, the everlasting truth of the Savior's conquest of death.

By the miracle of His rising from the dead, Jesus placed the seal of assurance upon the forgiveness of our sins. A dead Christ could not have been our Savior. An unopened grave would never have opened heaven. By breaking the chains of the tomb Jesus proved Himself to all ages the conqueror of sin. The sacrifice on Calvary had fulfilled its purpose; the ransom price paid for your sins and mine had been accepted by God. Hallelujah, what a Savior!

The open grave becomes the pledge of God that you and I, if we are believers in Christ, are going to live forever. The great problem of the human soul finds a solution at the empty tomb. In the Resurrection of Christ we learn that the short, perplexing life that is ours does not complete our destiny; the grave is not the end; we are not consigned to decay.

With the great stone rolled away from the entrance of Jesus' grave, every doubt and obstacle concerning our own eternity is removed.

So, in the radiance of Easter and in the power of Resurrection glory, may the Spirit of God bring into your own believing heart the assurance that you have the gift of eternal life. We who believe in Jesus Christ are able to say to the world, "Because He is risen, because He is alive, we too shall live!"

DISCUSSION AND REFLECTION

1. What convinces you to believe that Jesus really did rise from the dead?
2. We can be confident that through faith in Jesus Christ we have eternal life. How does knowing this affect the way you view death?
3. As Christians we celebrate the Resurrection every day as we walk in our new life with Jesus. What changes do you need to make to experience this new life more fully?

ADDITIONAL READING

JOHN 20:19-31

On the evening of that first day of the week, when the disciples were together, with the doors locked for fear of the Jews, Jesus came and stood among them and said, "Peace be with you!" After he said this, he showed them his hands and side. The disciples were overjoyed when they saw the Lord.

Again Jesus said, "Peace be with you! As the Father has sent me, I am sending you." And with that he breathed on them and said, "Receive the Holy Spirit. If you forgive anyone his sins, they are forgiven; if you do not forgive them, they are not forgiven."

Now Thomas (called Didymus), one of the Twelve, was not with the disciples when Jesus came. So the other disciples told him, "We have seen the Lord!"

But he said to them, "Unless I see the nail marks in his hands and put my finger where the nails were, and put my hand into his side, I will not believe it."

A week later his disciples were in the house again, and Thomas was with them. Though the doors were locked, Jesus came and stood among them and said, "Peace be with you!" Then he said to Thomas, "Put your finger here; see my hands. Reach out your hand and put it into my side. Stop doubting and believe."

Thomas said to him, "My Lord and my God!"

Then Jesus told him, "Because you have seen me, you have believed; blessed are those who have not seen and yet have believed."

Jesus did many other miraculous signs in the presence of his disciples, which are not recorded in this book. But these are written that you may believe that Jesus is the Christ, the Son of God, and that by believing you may have life in his name.

We are not to regard the cross as defeat and the resurrection as victory. Rather, the cross was victory won, and the resurrection the victory endorsed, proclaimed and demonstrated.

John R. W. Stott, The Cross of Christ

I know of no one fact in the history of mankind which is proved by better evidence of every sort, to the understanding of a fair enquirer, than the great sign which God has given us that Christ died and rose again from the dead.

Thomas Arnold, 1795-1842

JOHN 11:25

I am the resurrection and the life. He who believes in me will live, even though he dies; and whoever lives and believes in me will never die.

WERE YOU THERE?

Were you there when they crucified my Lord?
Were you there when they crucified my Lord?
O! Sometimes it causes me to tremble, tremble, tremble.
Were you there when they crucified my Lord?

Were you there when they nailed Him to the tree?
Were you there when they nailed Him to the tree?
O! Sometimes it causes me to tremble, tremble, tremble.
Were you there when they nailed Him to the tree?

Were you there when they laid Him in the tomb?
Were you there when they laid Him in the tomb?
O! Sometimes it causes me to tremble, tremble, tremble.
Were you there when they laid Him in the tomb?

Were you there when He rose up from the grave?
Were you there when He rose up from the grave?
O! Sometimes it causes me to tremble, tremble, tremble.
Were you there when He rose up from the grave?

Anonymous, American Folk Melody

FAMILY ACTIVITIES

Consider using the material in this session for a family sunrise service. Decide on a place outside where you can go to watch the sun rise as you read and pray together as a family. Then plan a special breakfast together.

□ □ □

As you gather with extended family and friends for Easter dinner, have each child share what he or she most enjoyed in your devotional times as a family this past week.

□ □ □

Complete the last section of your Picture Poster. Have the children write out the words "He Lives" in colorful letters. (For small children, an adult can draw block letters for the child to color.)

□ □ □

There are many traditional foods associated with Christmas. You may want to establish some unique foods that your family will look forward to eating on Easter. Some cultures have a fancy sweet bread called Easter Bread. Perhaps you have a special food that you would like to use in connection with Easter.

□ □ □

Have each family member write a short letter to himself. Include some of the things that have meant a lot to you this Easter, and some spiritual goals you hope to achieve in the next year. Small children can dictate to an adult.

Place these letters in a sealed envelope. Put the envelope away, along with the pictures and writings you did during your activity times this week. Store them until next Easter. Your children will love looking back at what they wrote a year earlier, and seeing how their drawing and writing have improved. (It might be helpful to make a note in this book about where you put these Easter materials, before you put this book on the shelf.)

WHO OVERCAME EVIL BY GOOD

They stretch Him
On a Cross to die—
Our Lord Who first
Stretched out the sky

Whose countenance
The cherubim
Dare not gaze on . . .
They spat on Him

And gave Him gall
    to drink
Though He
Brings us wells
Of eternity.

He prays for them
"Father, forgive . . ."
For He was born
That all might live.

Round the sealed tomb
Of Him they've slain
They set a guard
In vain, in vain

Round Him
Creation can't contain,
Who dies for us
To rise again.

M. Whitcomb Hess, Author
After a homily by Saint Amphilochius, fourth century
Copyright 1981 CHRISTIANITY TODAY, used by permission.

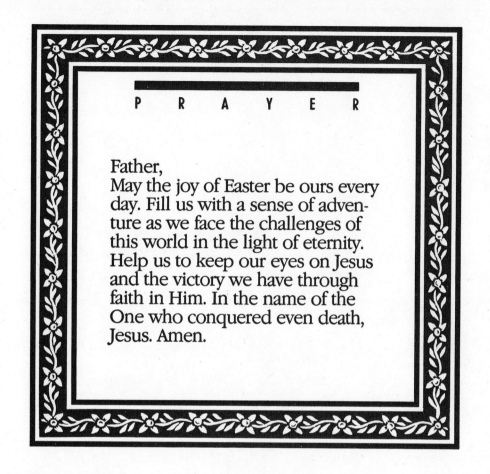

PRAYER

Father,
May the joy of Easter be ours every day. Fill us with a sense of adventure as we face the challenges of this world in the light of eternity. Help us to keep our eyes on Jesus and the victory we have through faith in Him. In the name of the One who conquered even death, Jesus. Amen.